GIRL STUFF

24 PAGE COLORING BOOK

FOR KARYN ROMANO
who loved to color and brought color to the world

ROO PUBLISHING

Illustrations by Dani Kates

Dear Colorer,

My name is Dani and I drew the pictures in this coloring book!
I'm an artist, a designer, and a HUGE fan of coloring.
When I buy a coloring book, the first thing I do is take a thin black pen and draw tiny detailed lines and patterns to make the pictures more fun to color. I love doing it so much that I decided to design my own coloring books with the same type of detailed lines and fun patterns.

All of those details and lines make this is an "adult" style coloring book, but the pictures are way more fun to color!

This one is all about Girly stuff, like nail polish, shopping, baking, and fashion.

So have fun, color something amazing and share it with me on social media!
@ColorWithDani
#ColorWithDani

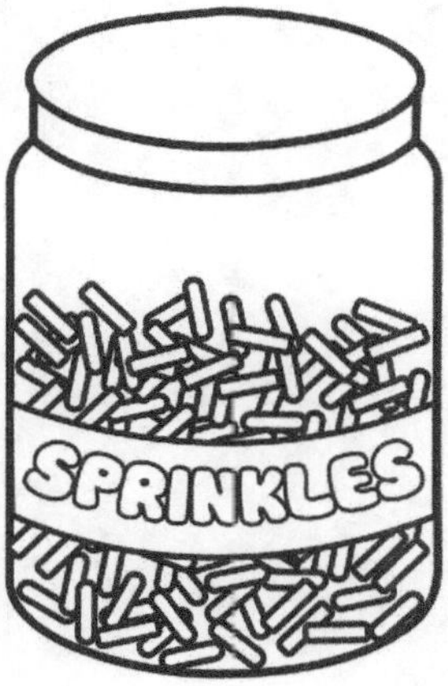

XOXO,
Dani Kates

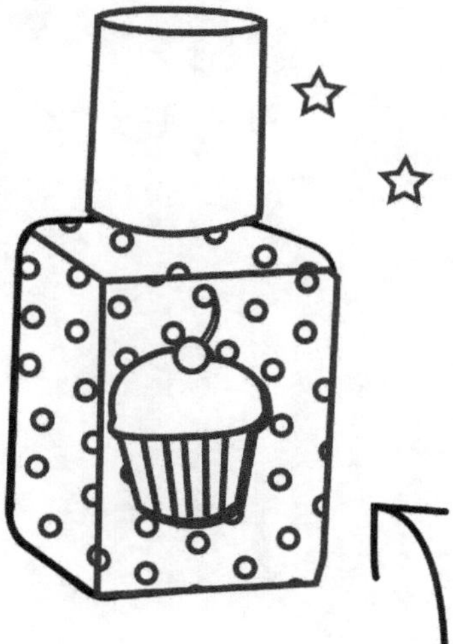

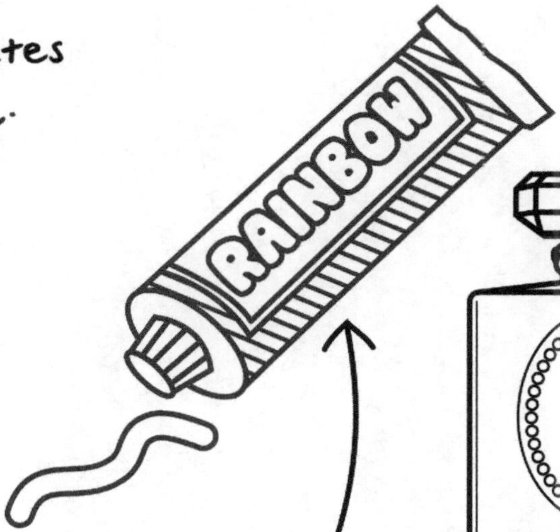

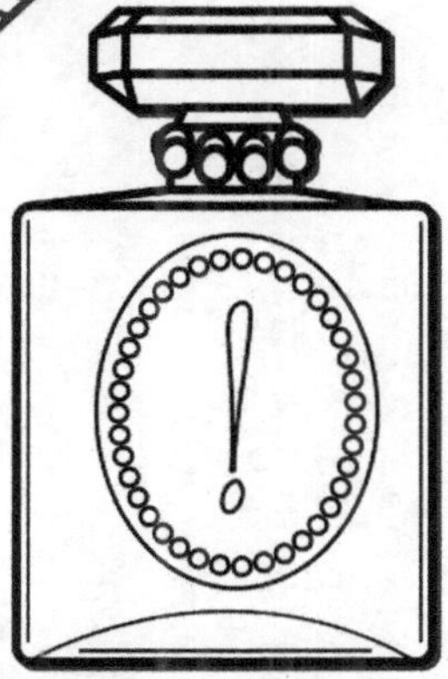

P.S. These are some of my favorite pictures in this book!

ROO PUBLISHING

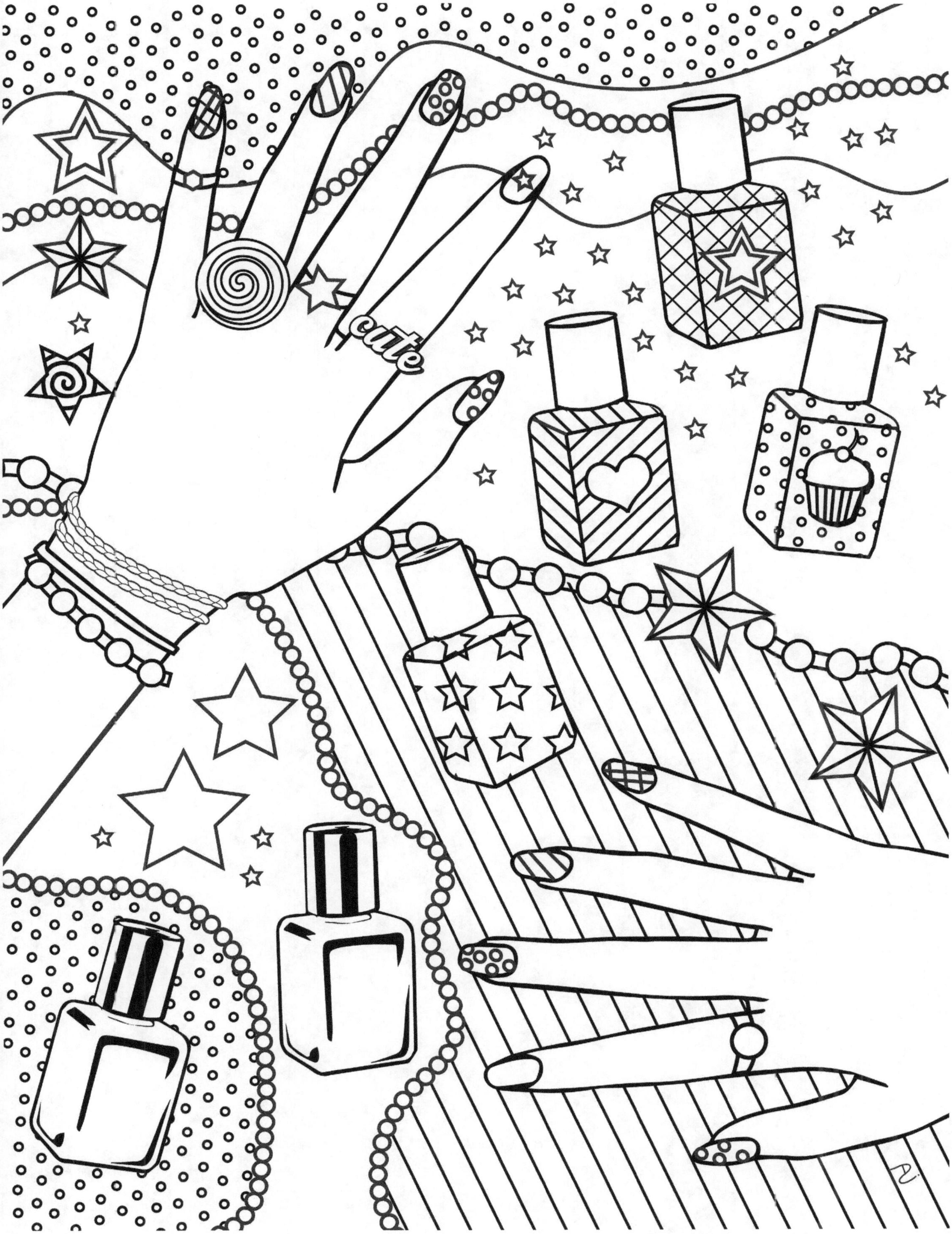
cute

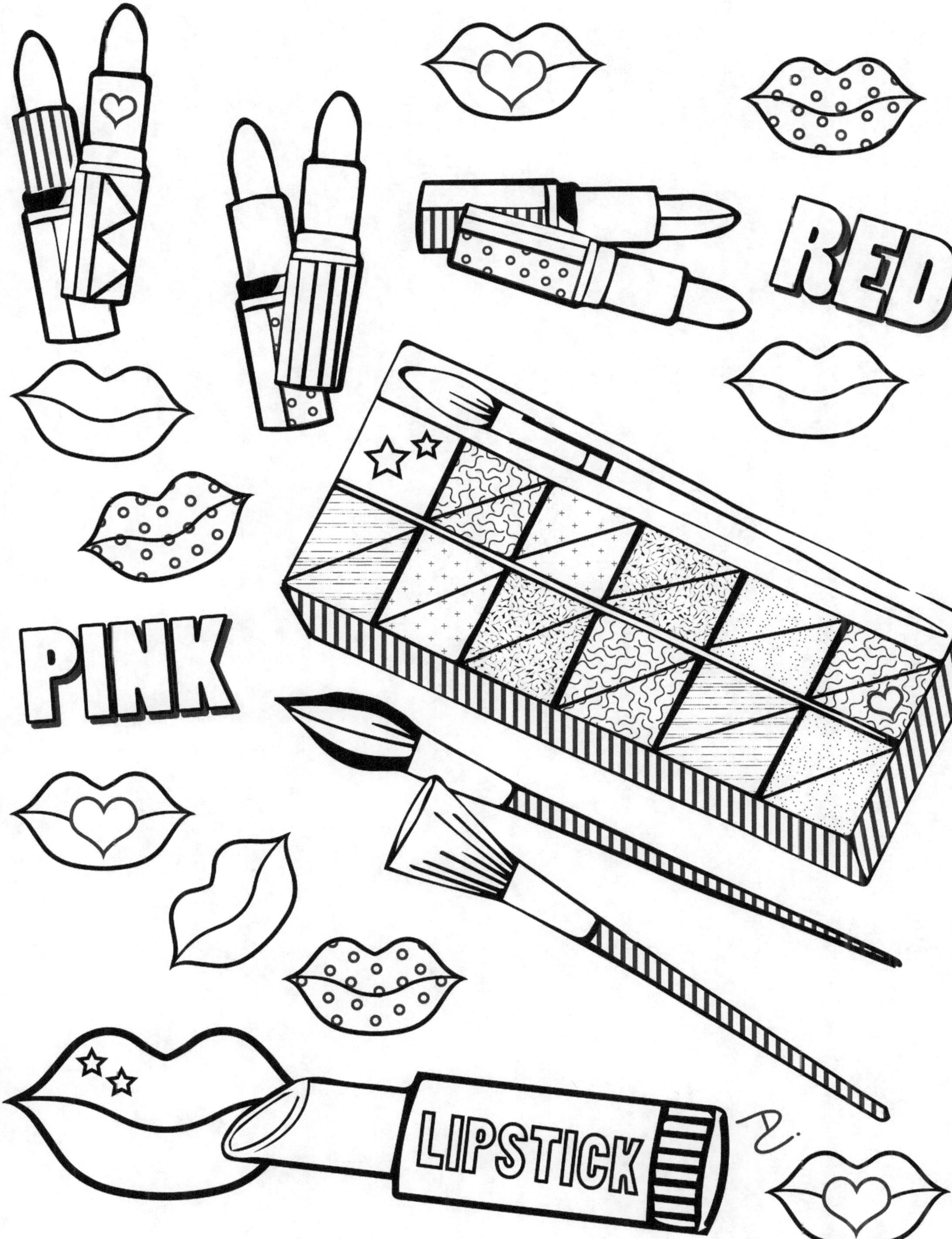
RED
PINK
LIPSTICK

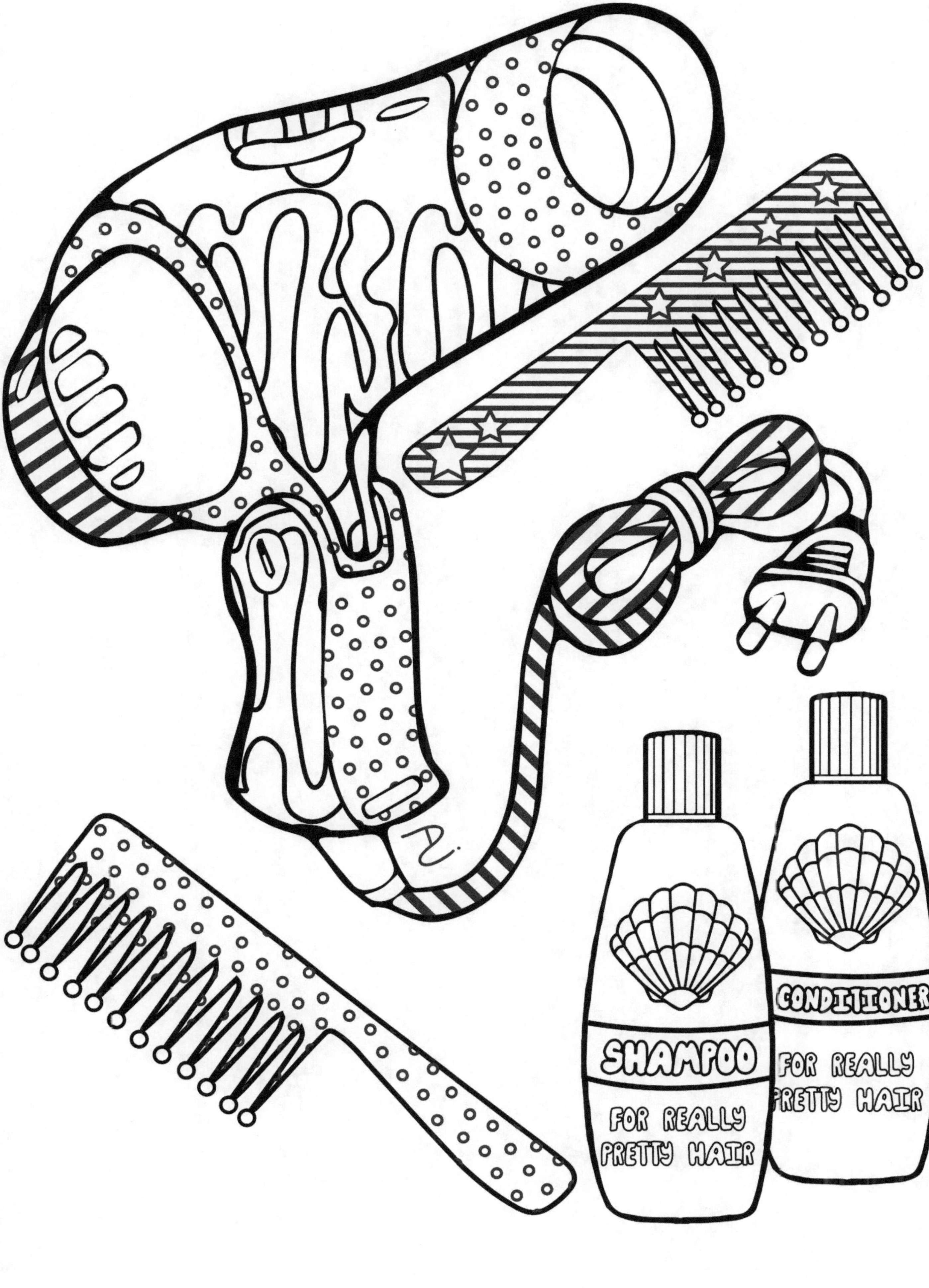
SHAMPOO
FOR REALLY PRETTY HAIR
CONDITIONER
FOR REALLY PRETTY HAIR

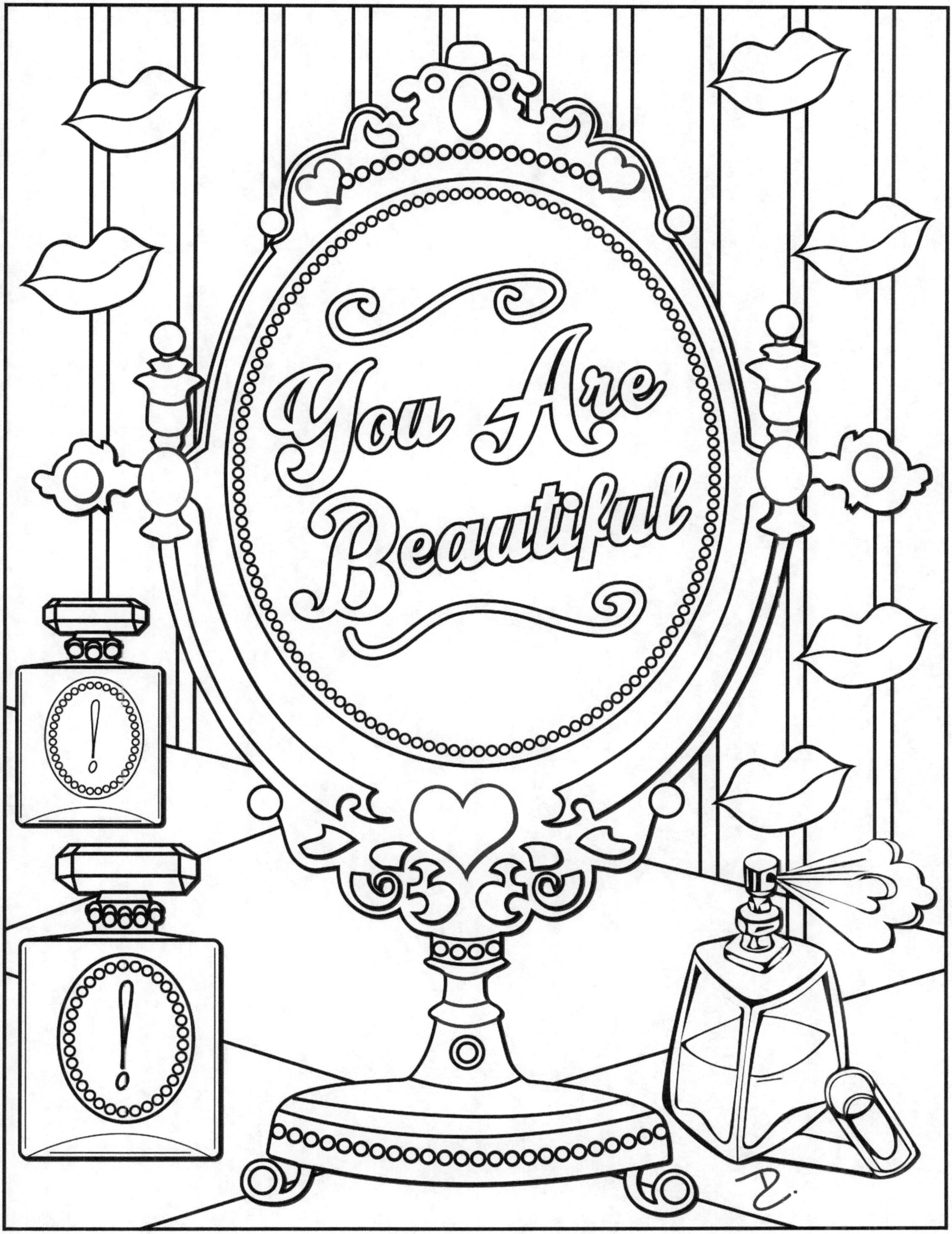
You Are Beautiful

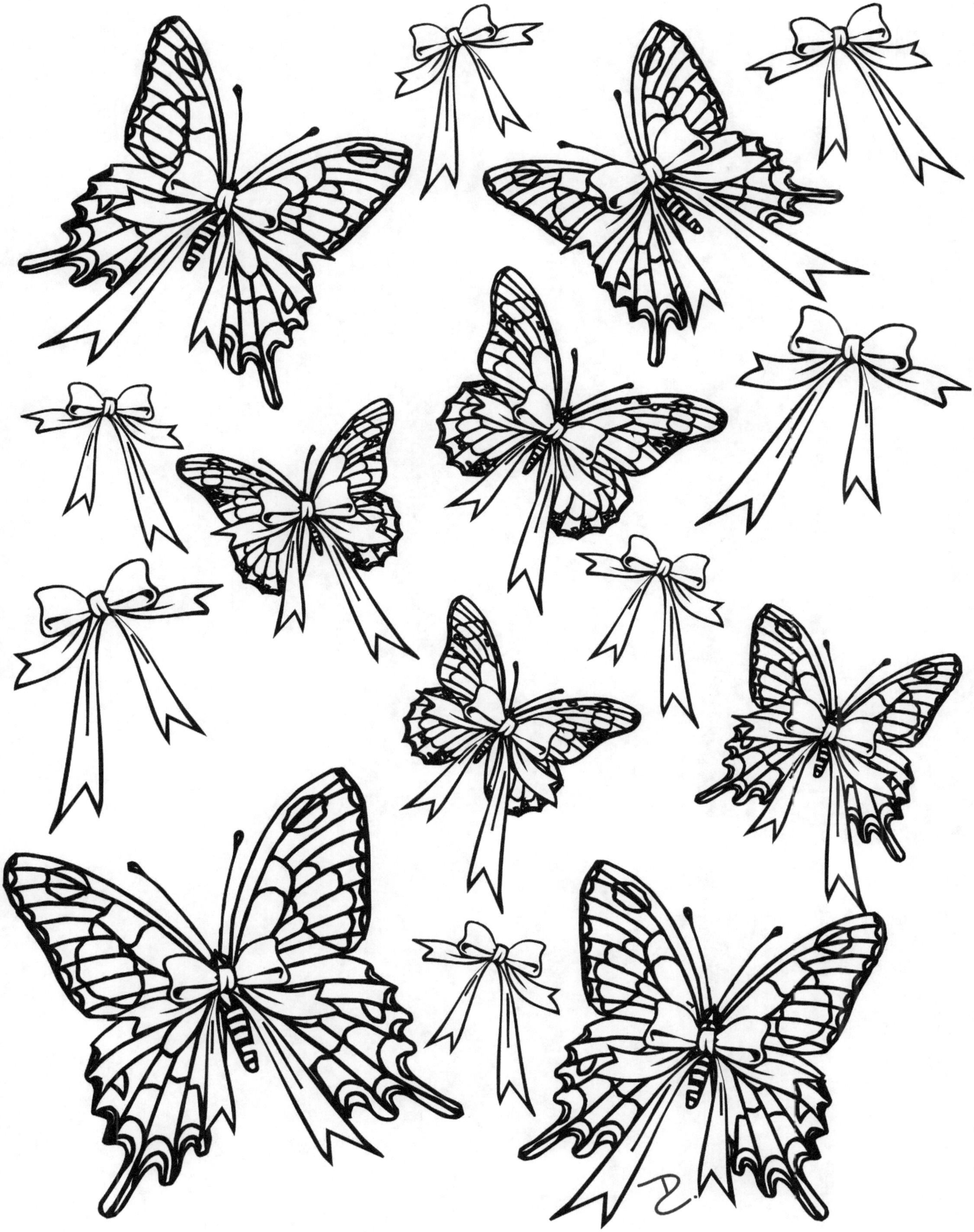

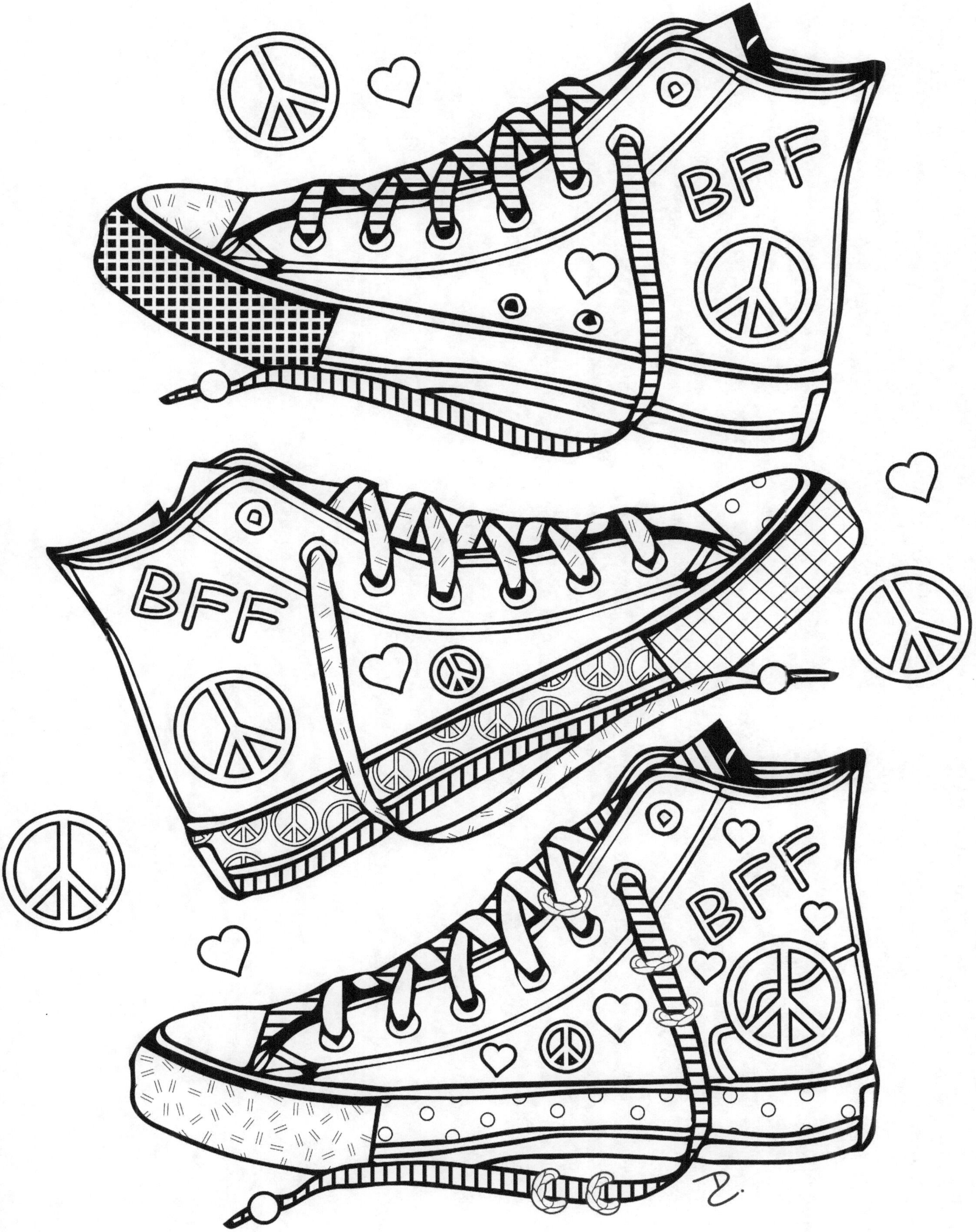
BFF
BFF
BFF

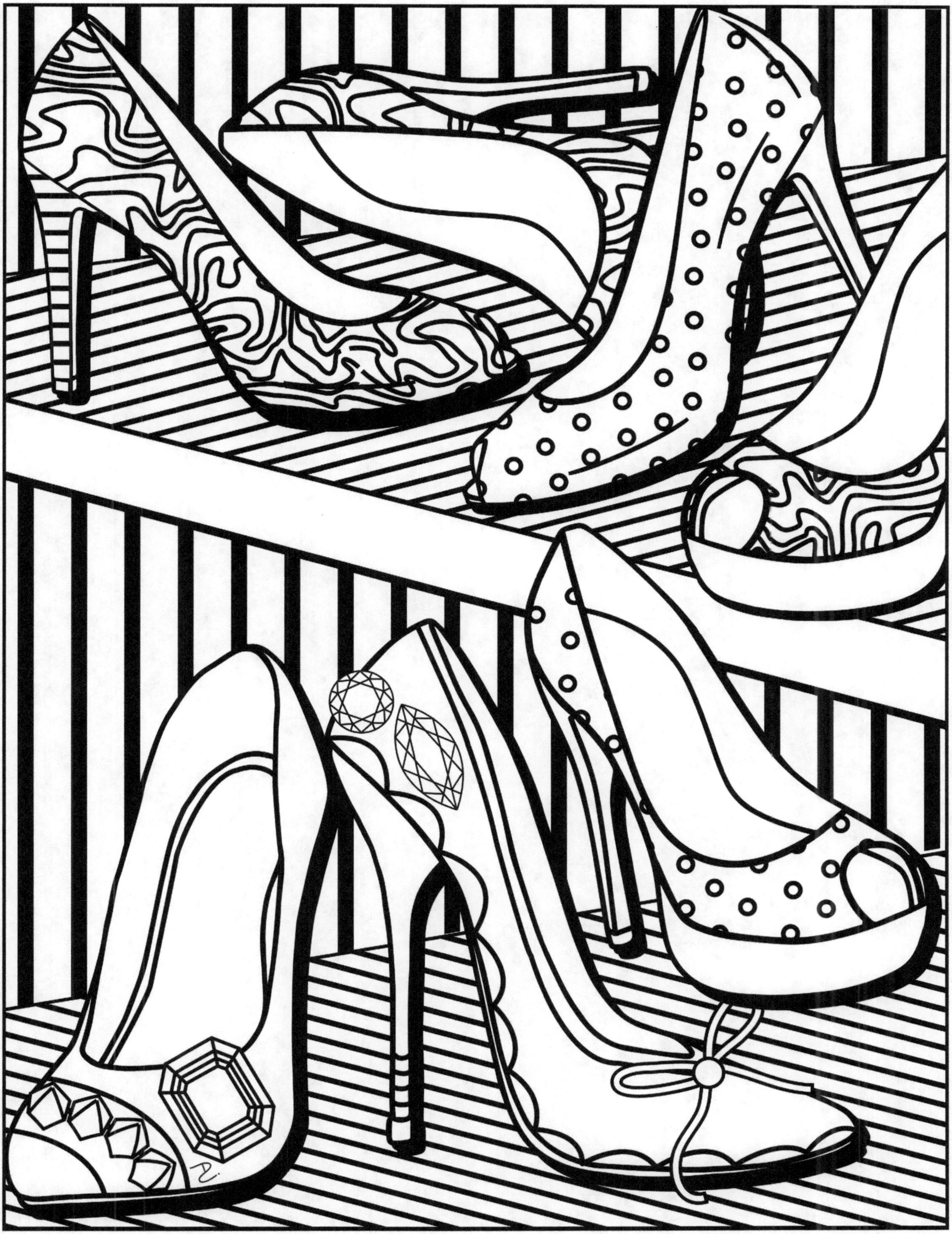

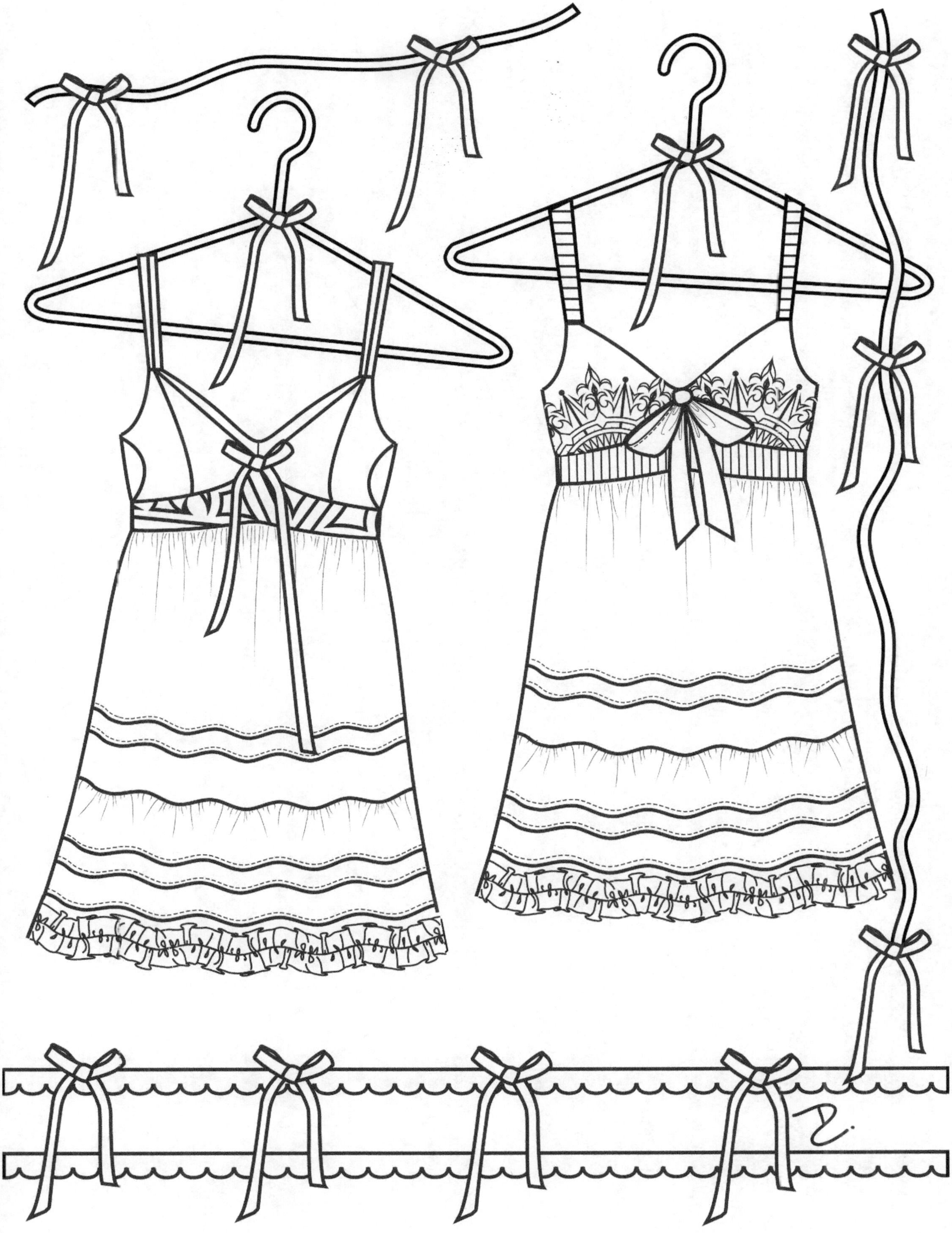

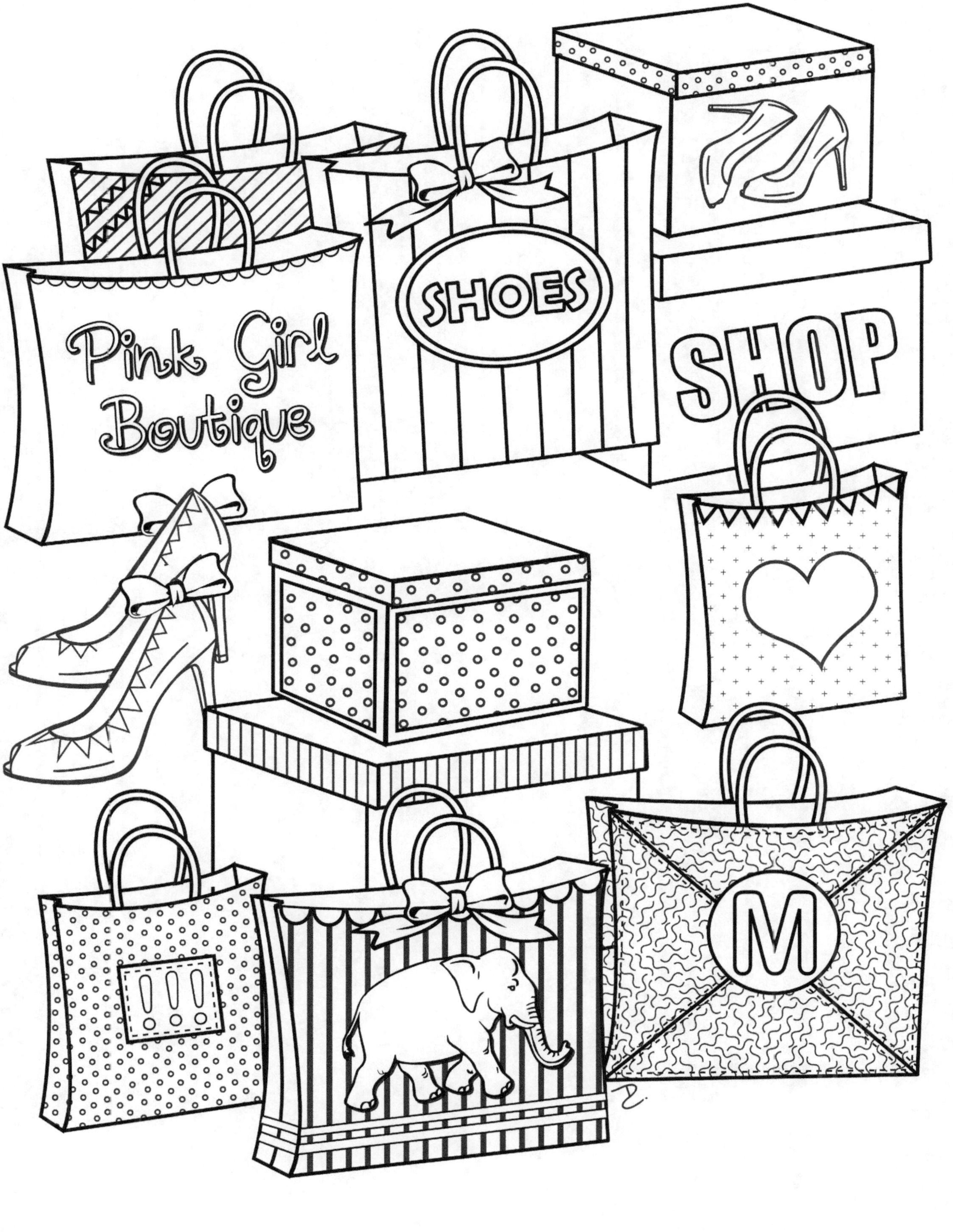

SHOES
Pink Girl Boutique
SHOP
!!!
M

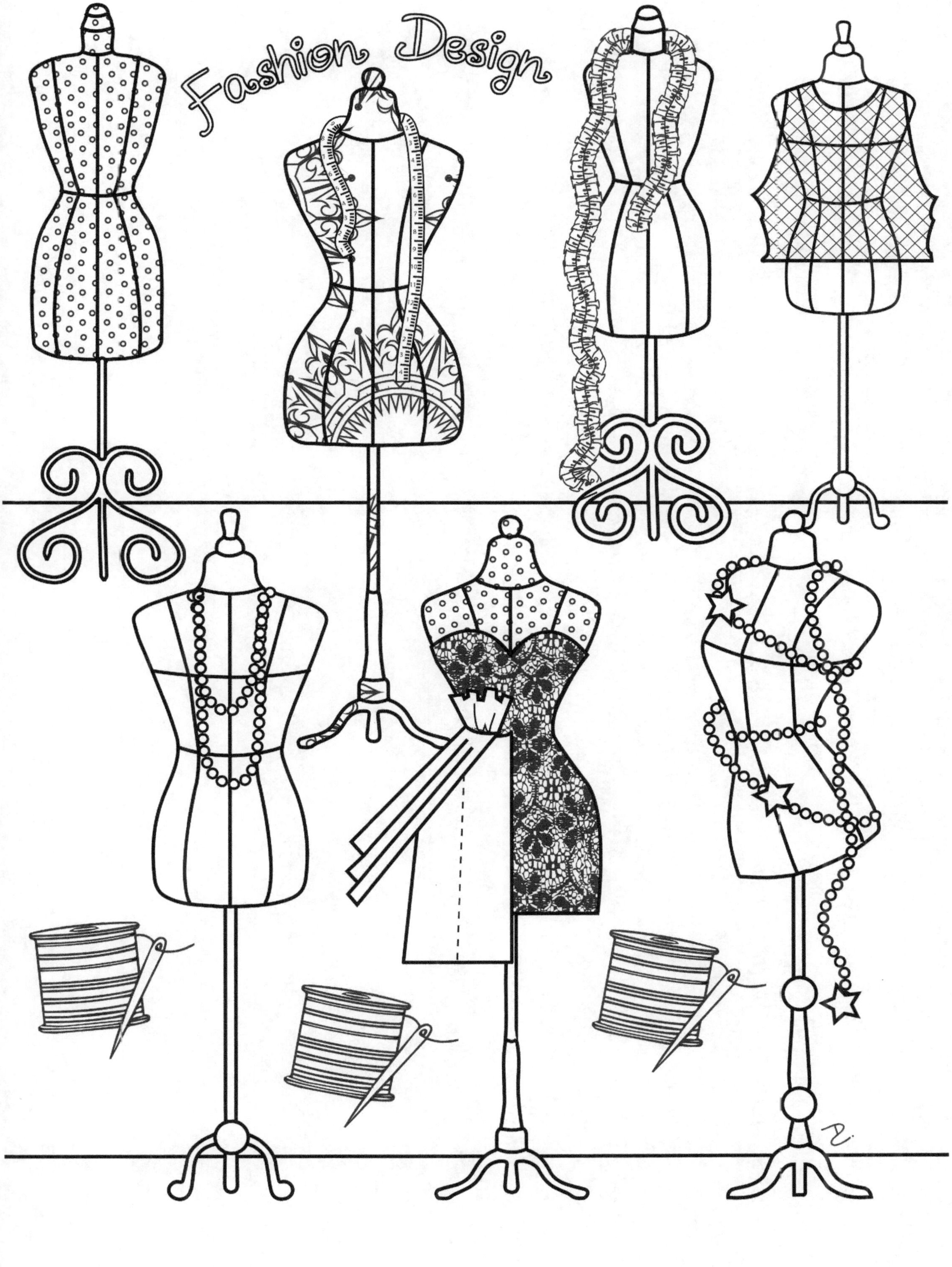
Fashion Design

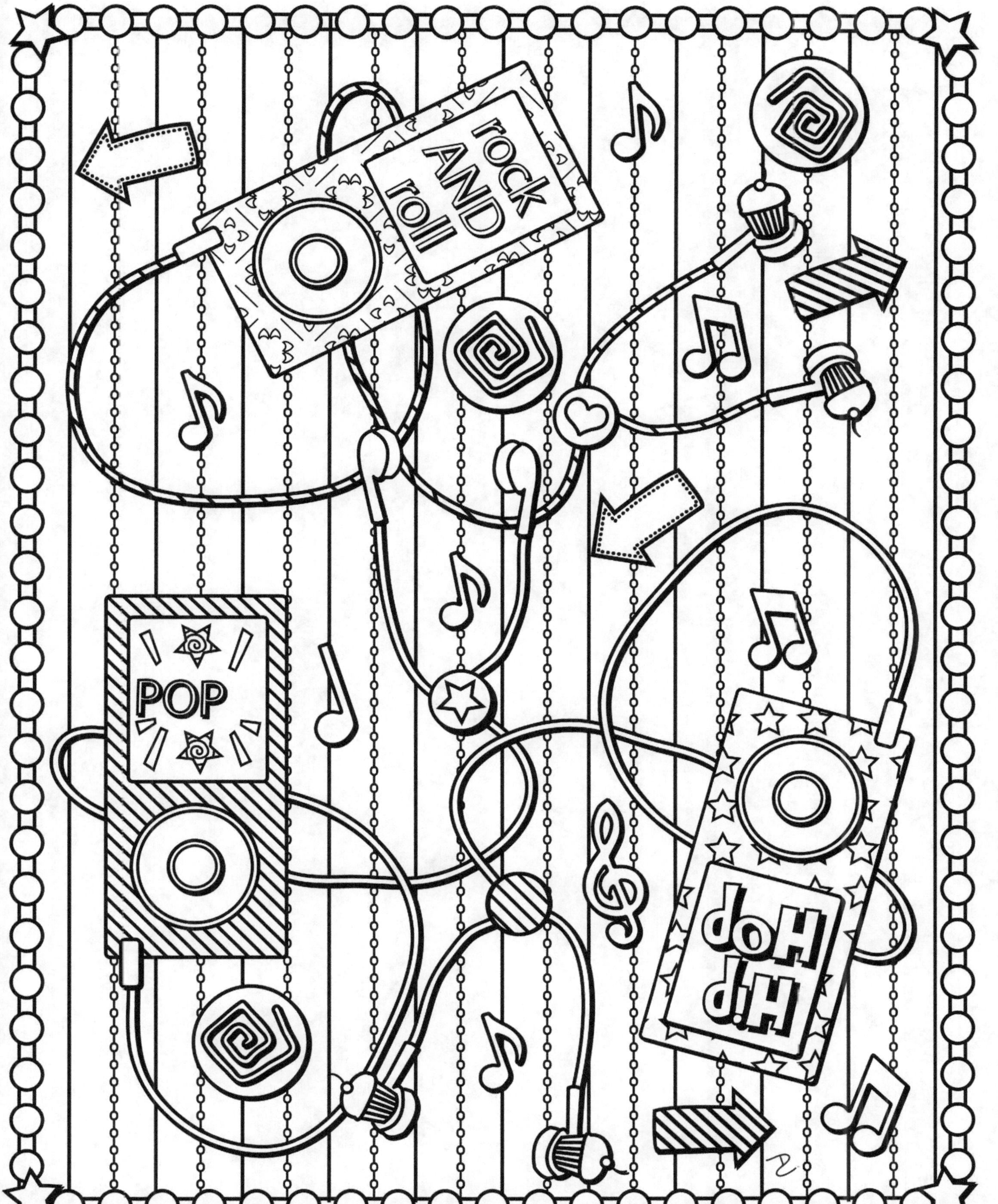
rock AND roll
POP
Hip Hop

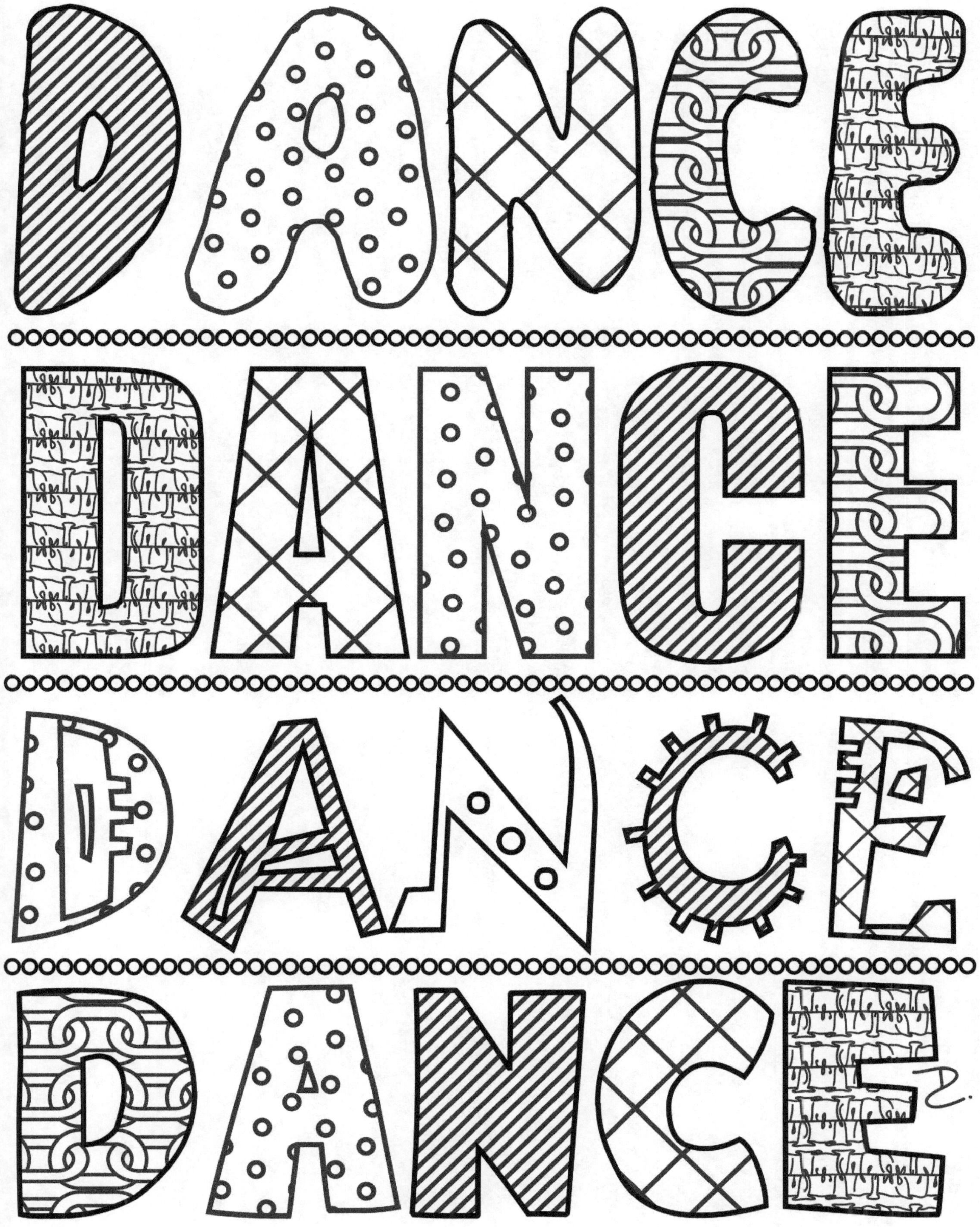
DANCE
DANCE
DANCE
DANCE

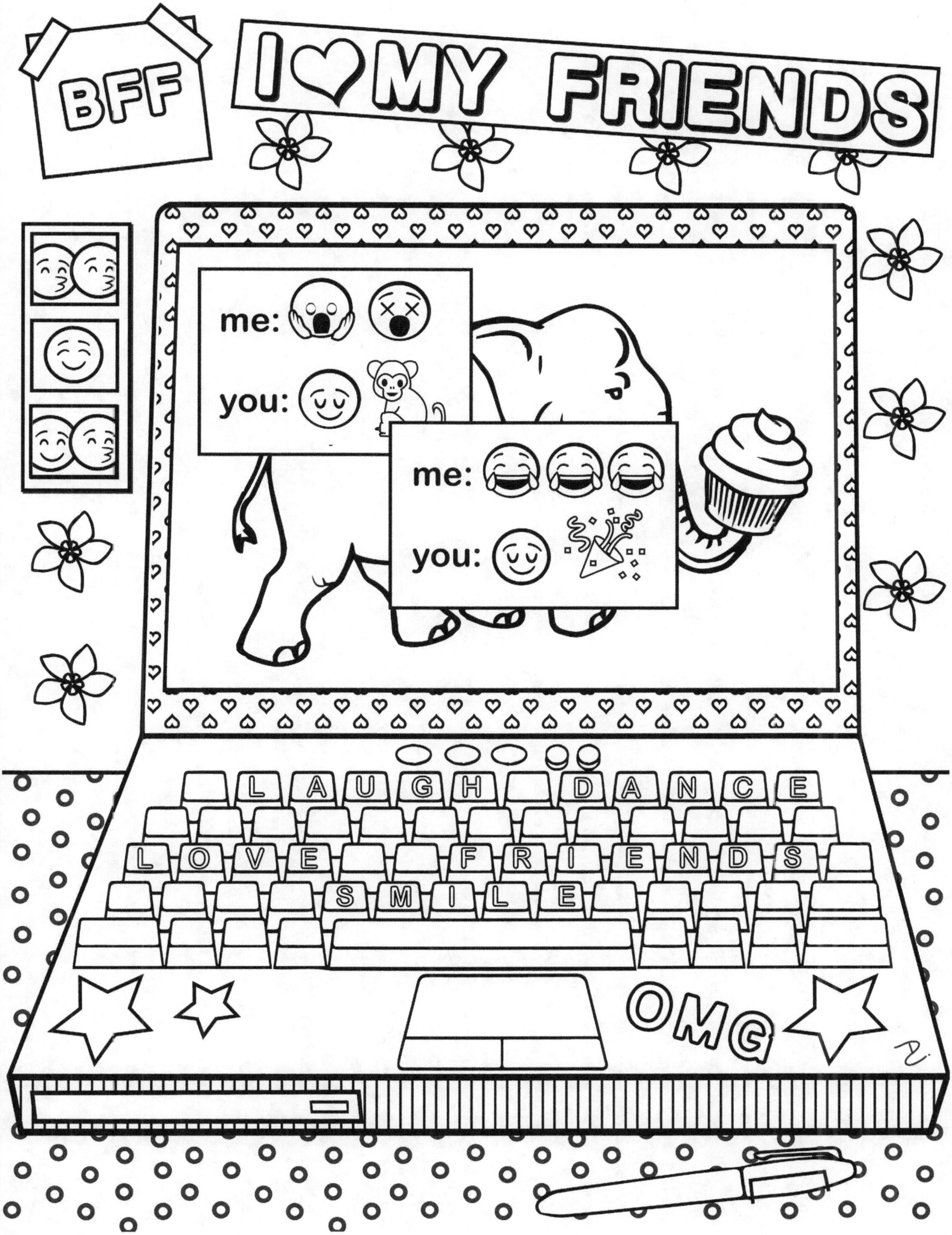
BFF
I ♥ MY FRIENDS
me:
you:
me:
you:
LAUGH DANCE
LOVE FRIENDS
SMILE
OMG

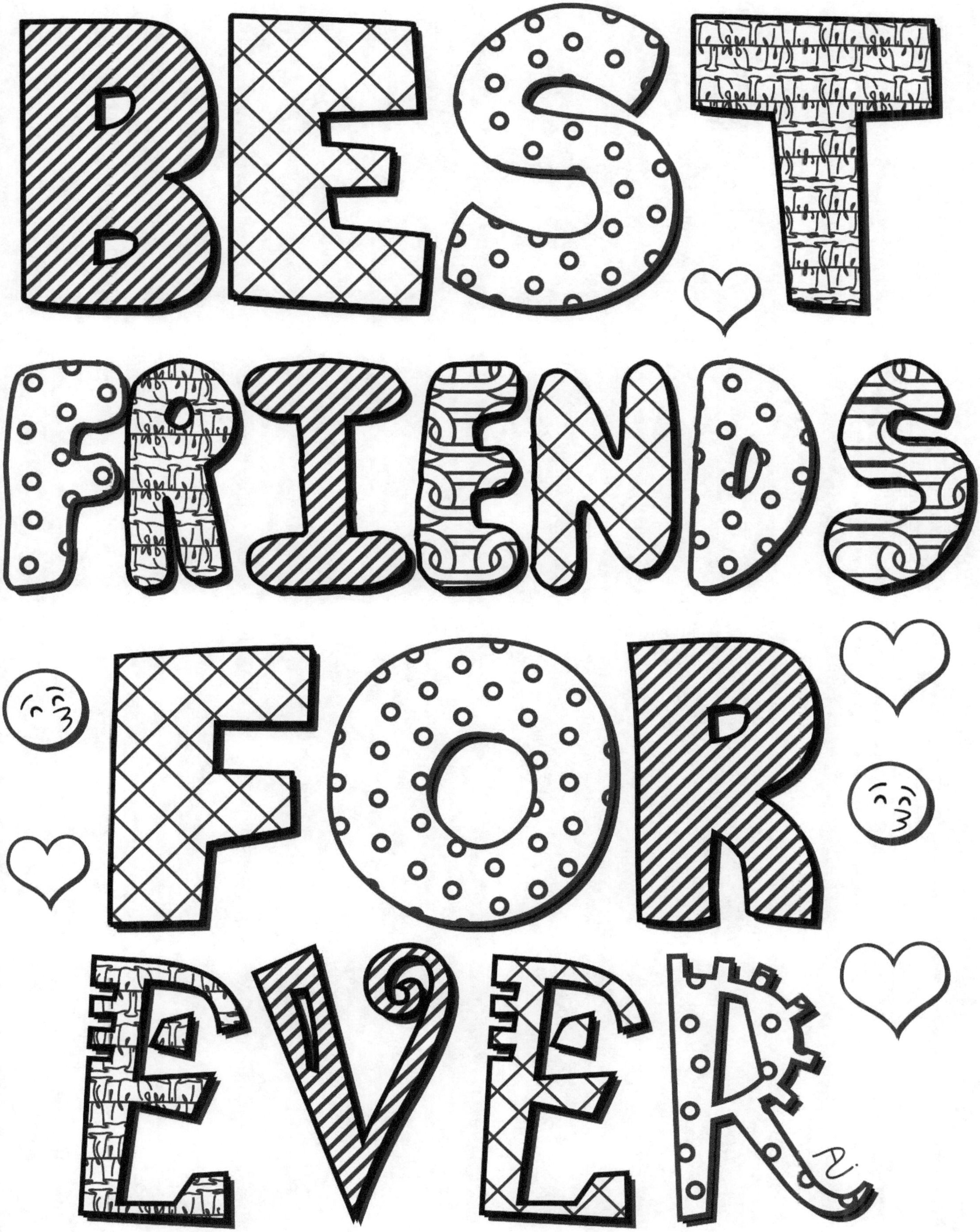
BEST
FRIENDS
FOR
EVER

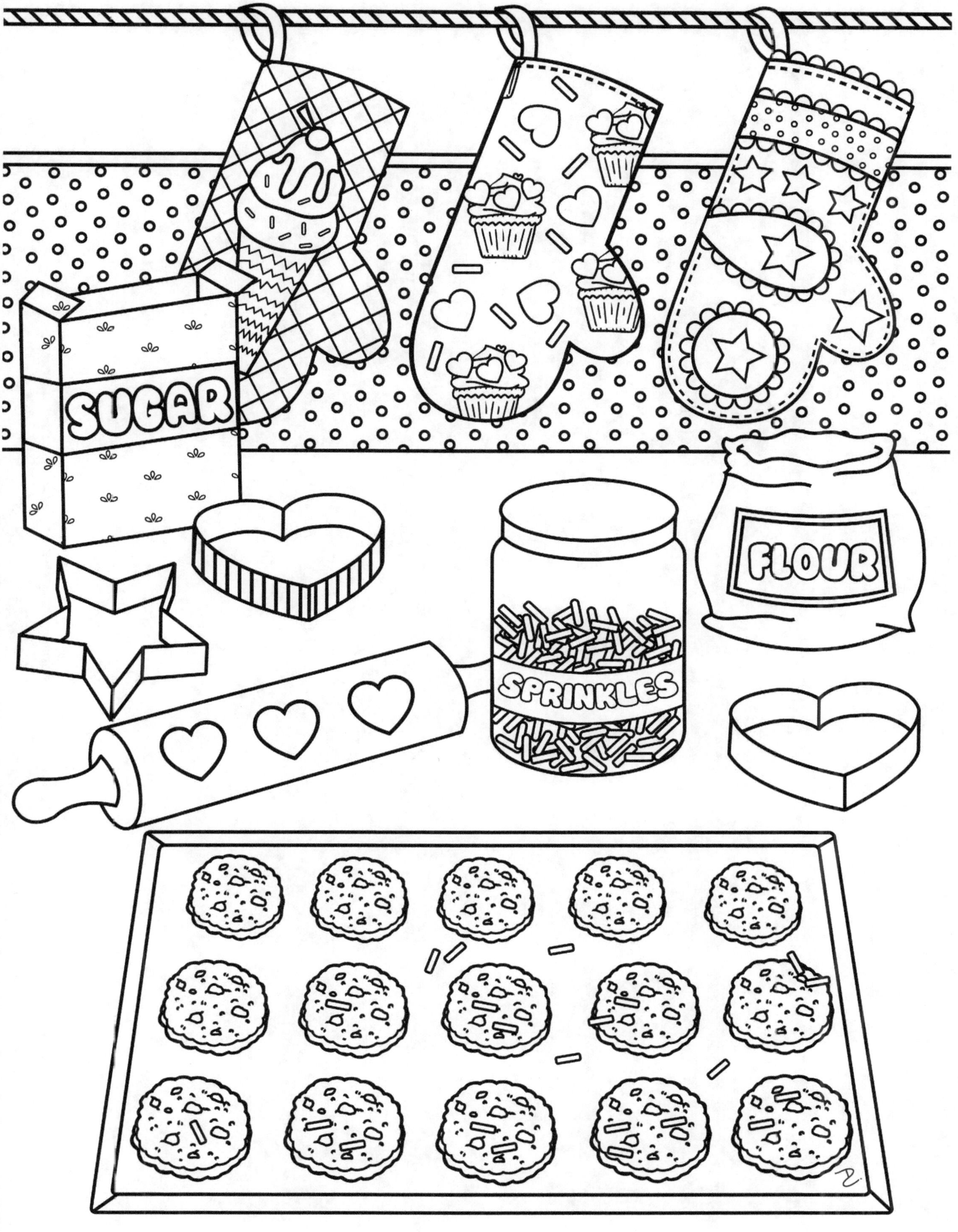

SUGAR
FLOUR
SPRINKLES

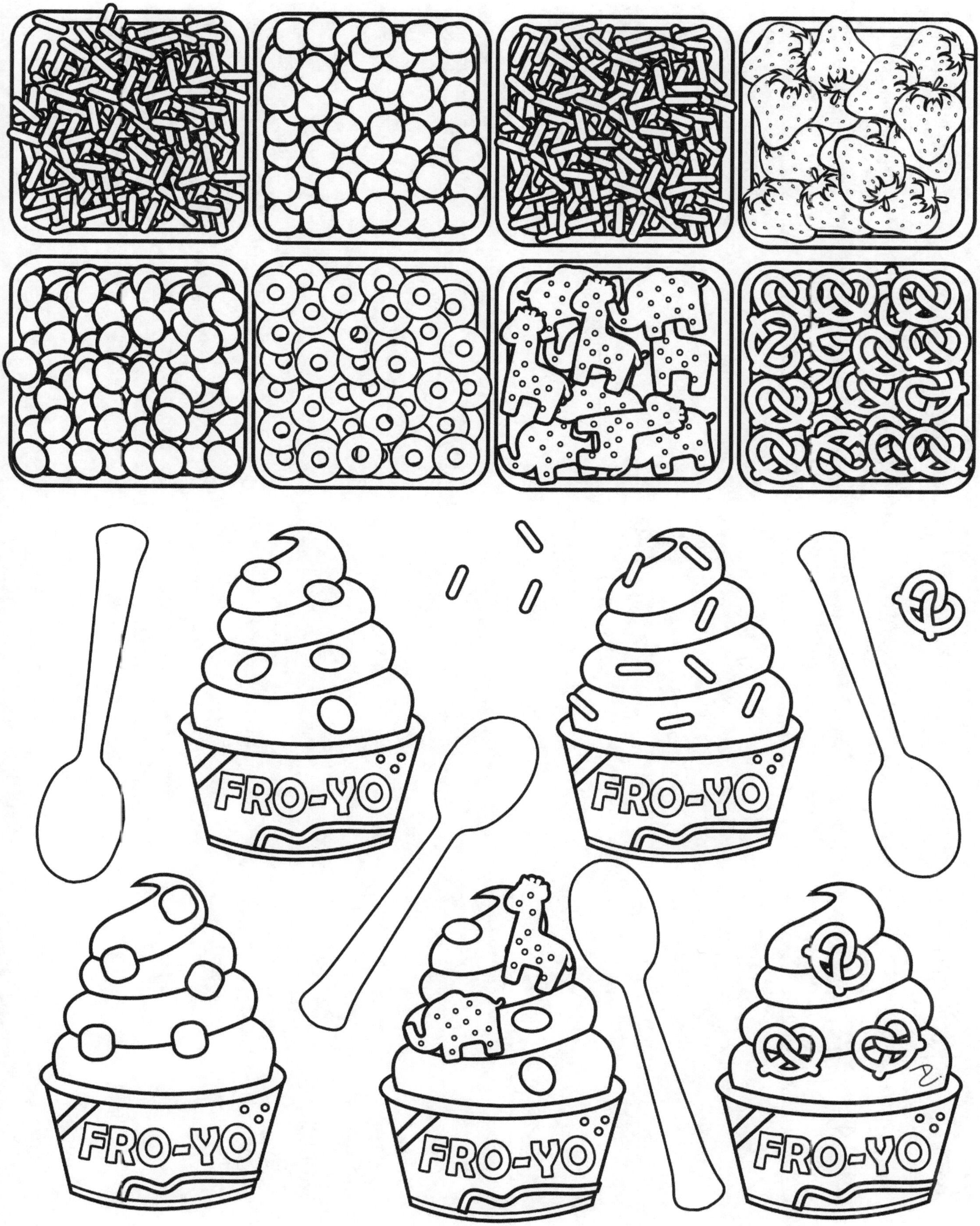

FRO-YO
FRO-YO
FRO-YO
FRO-YO
FRO-YO

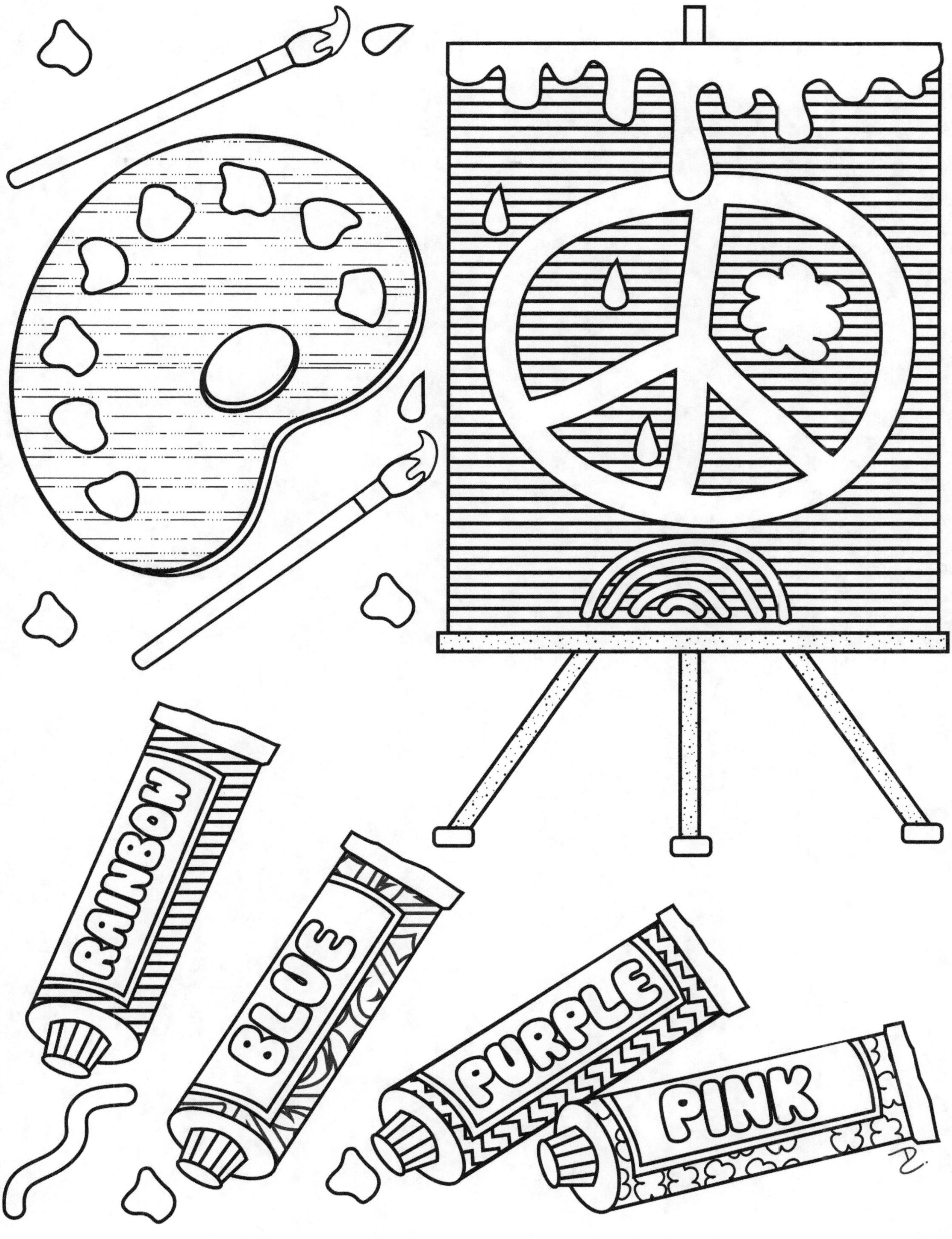
RAINBOW
BLUE
PURPLE
PINK

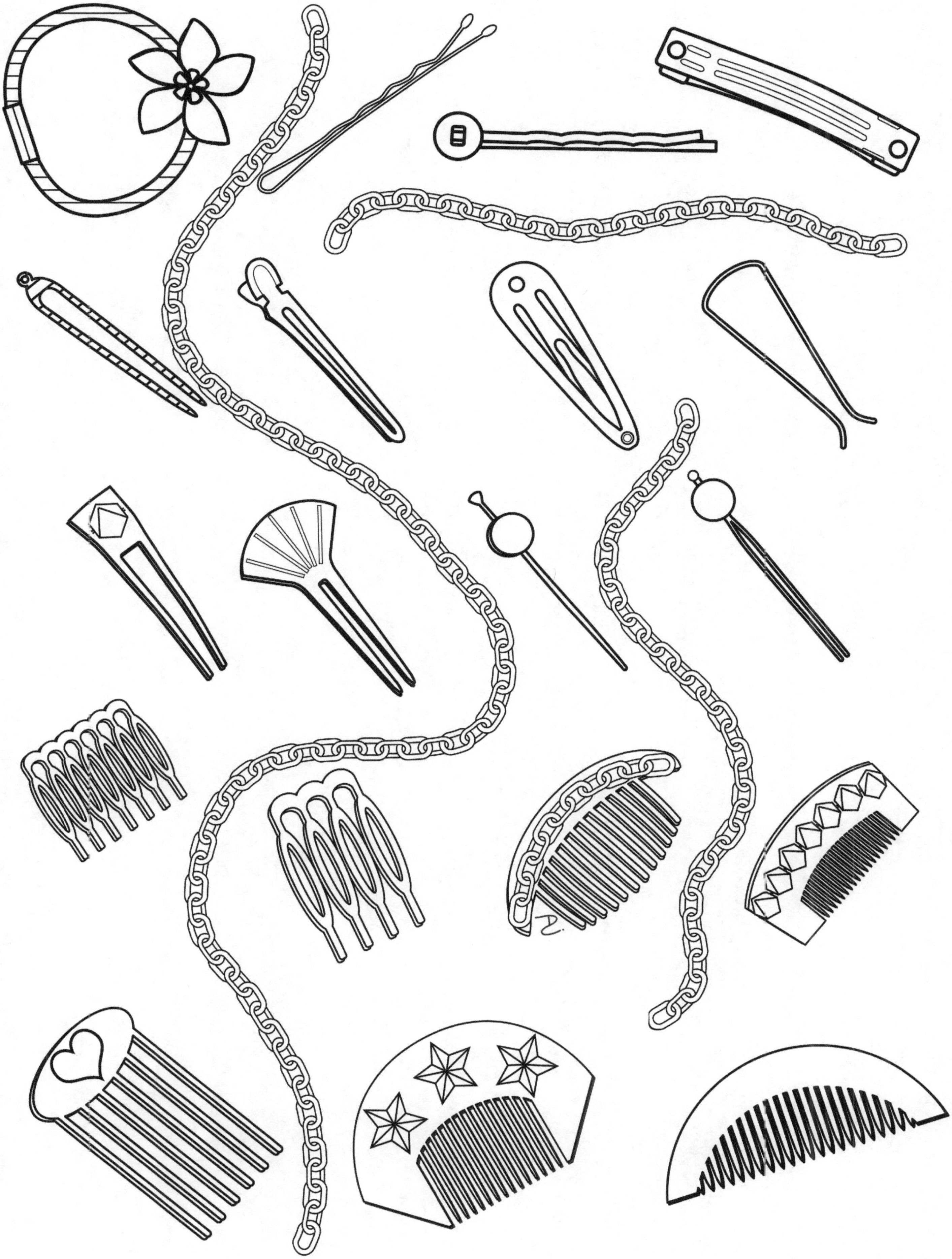

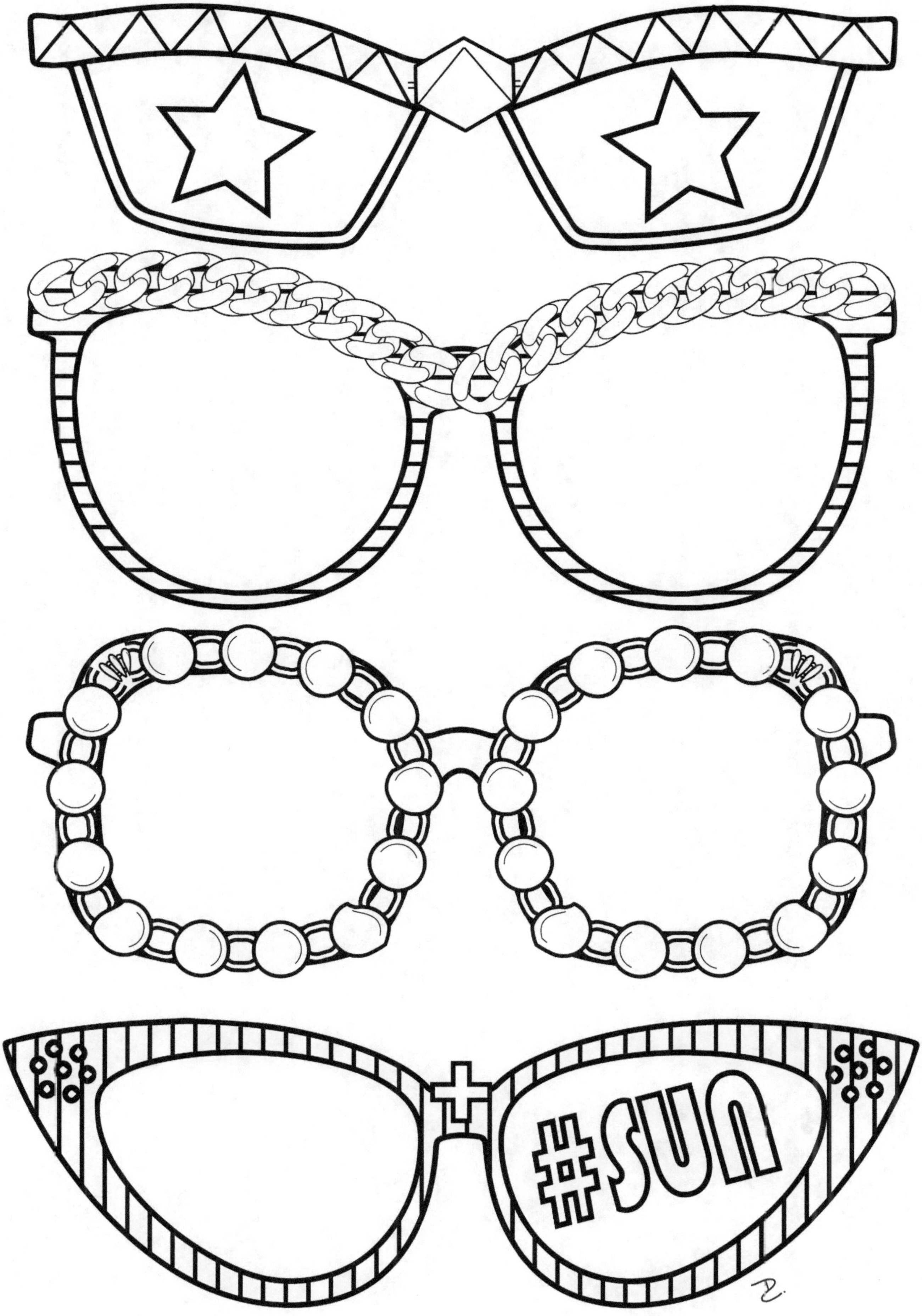
#SUN

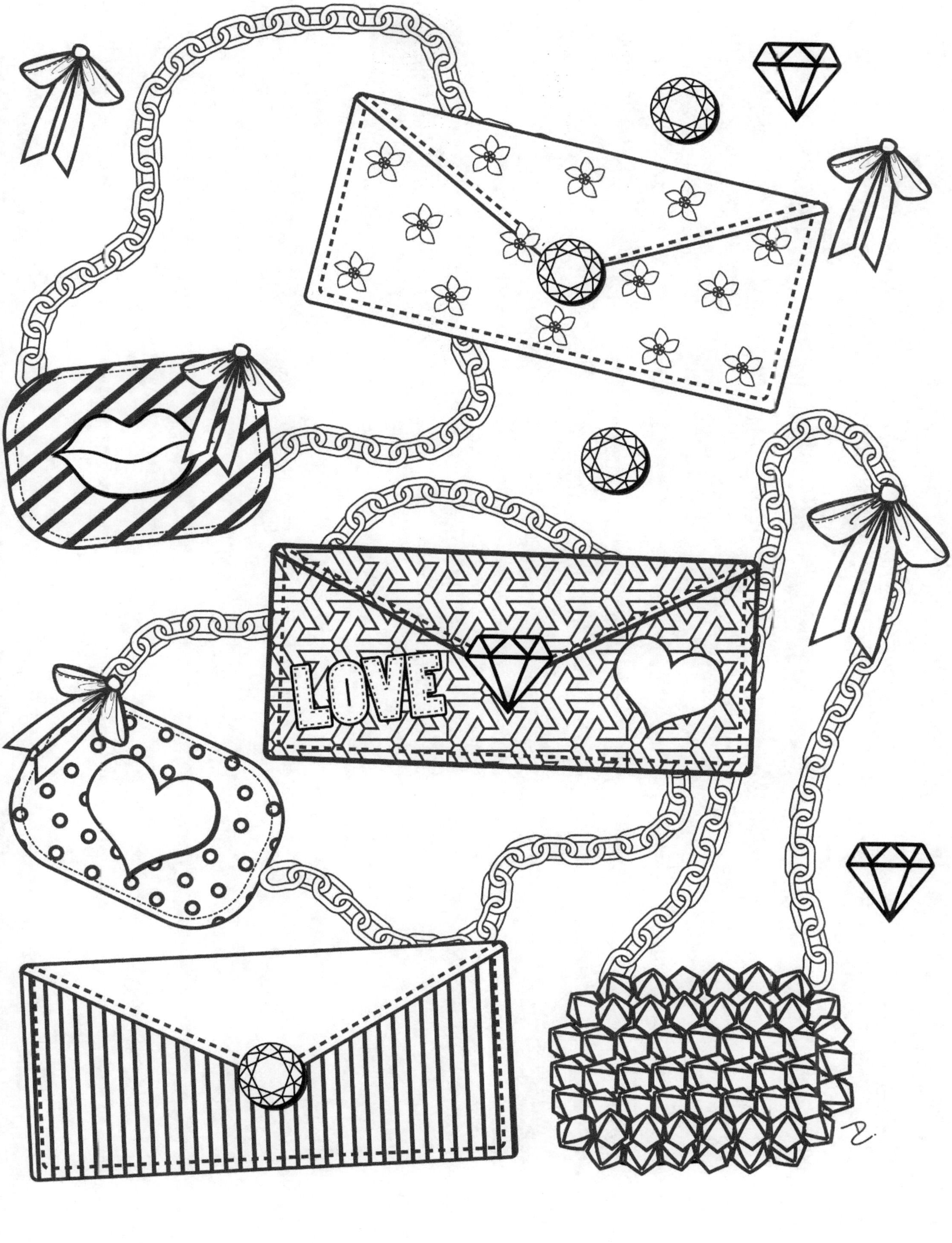
LOVE

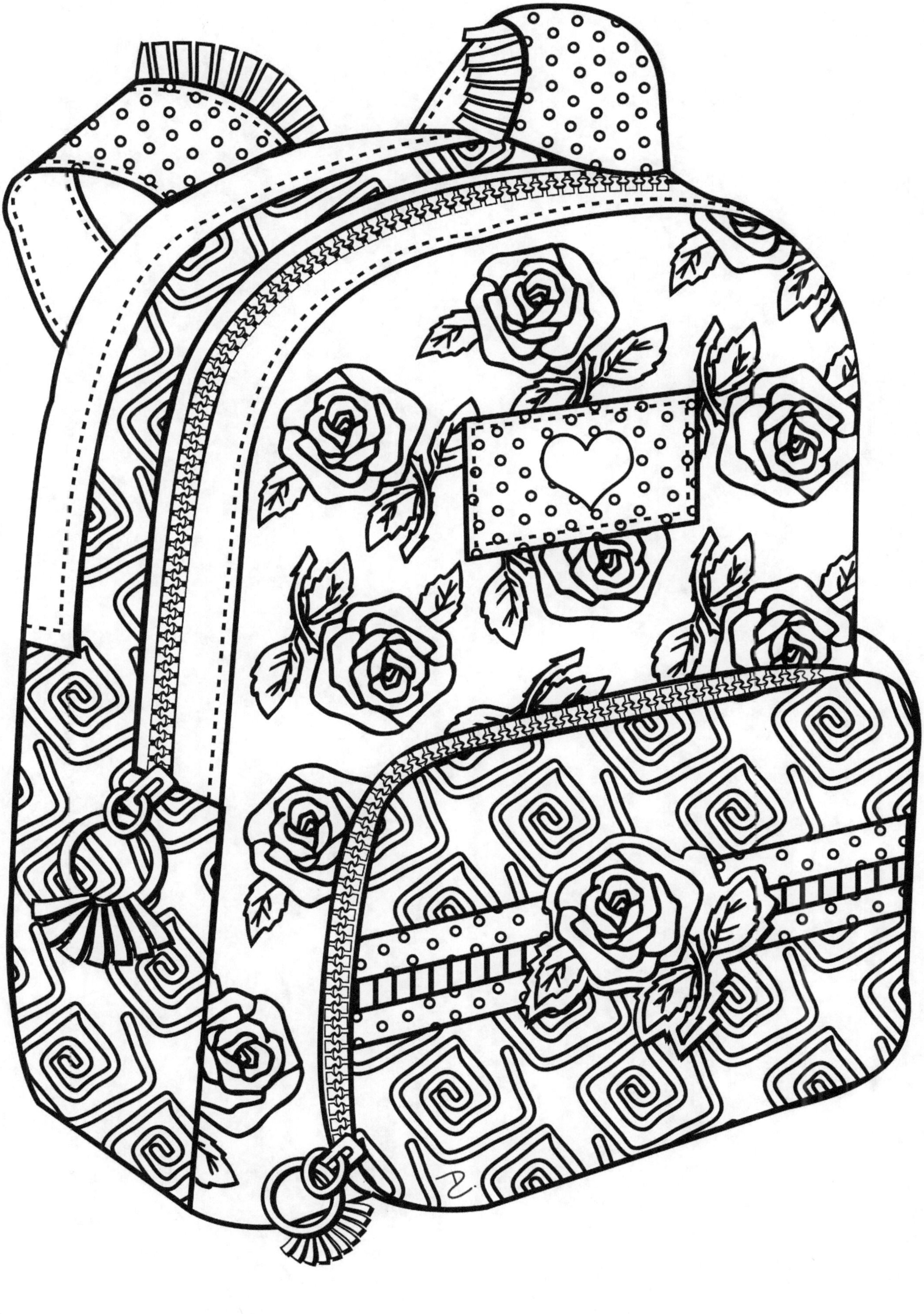

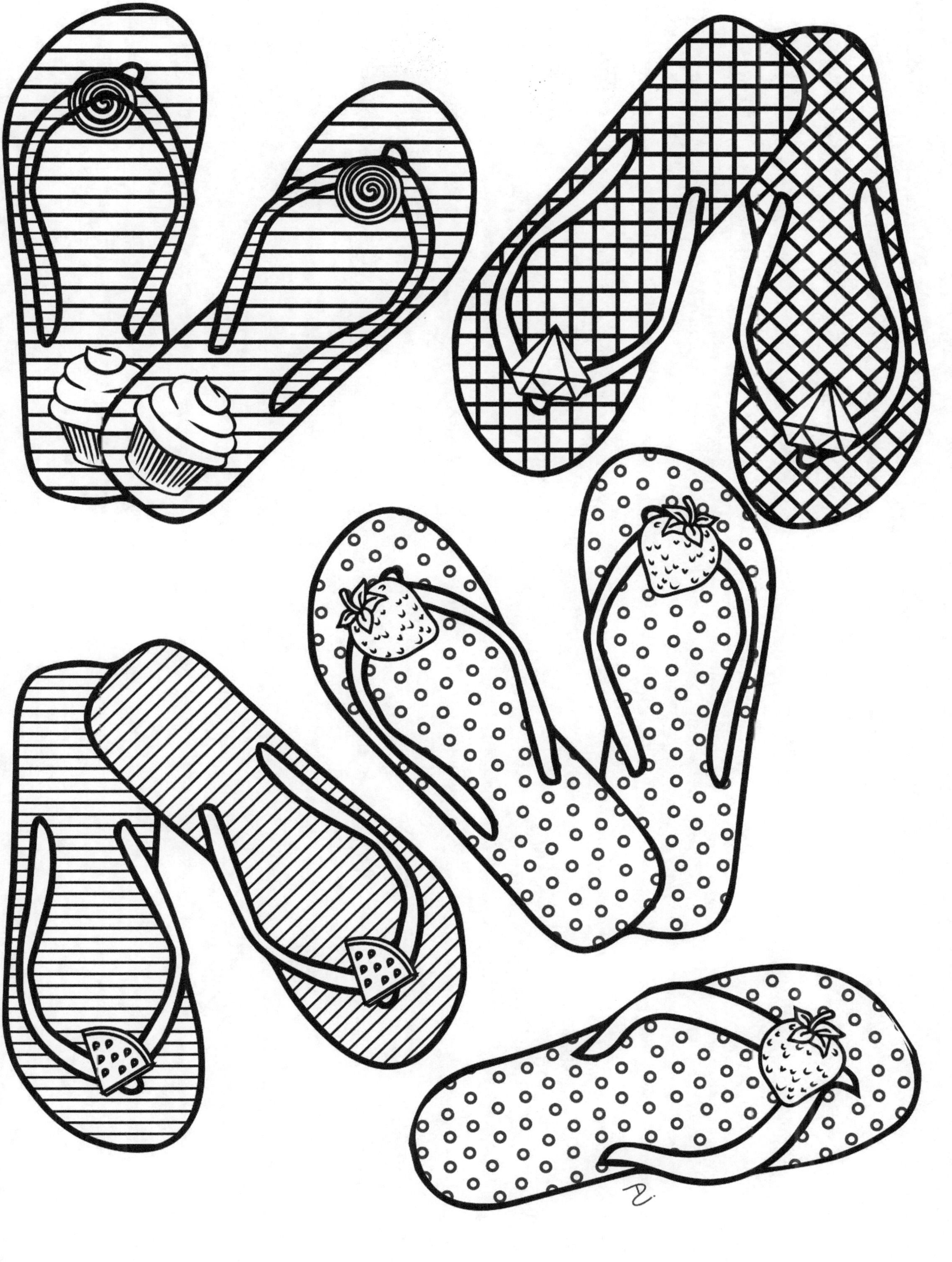

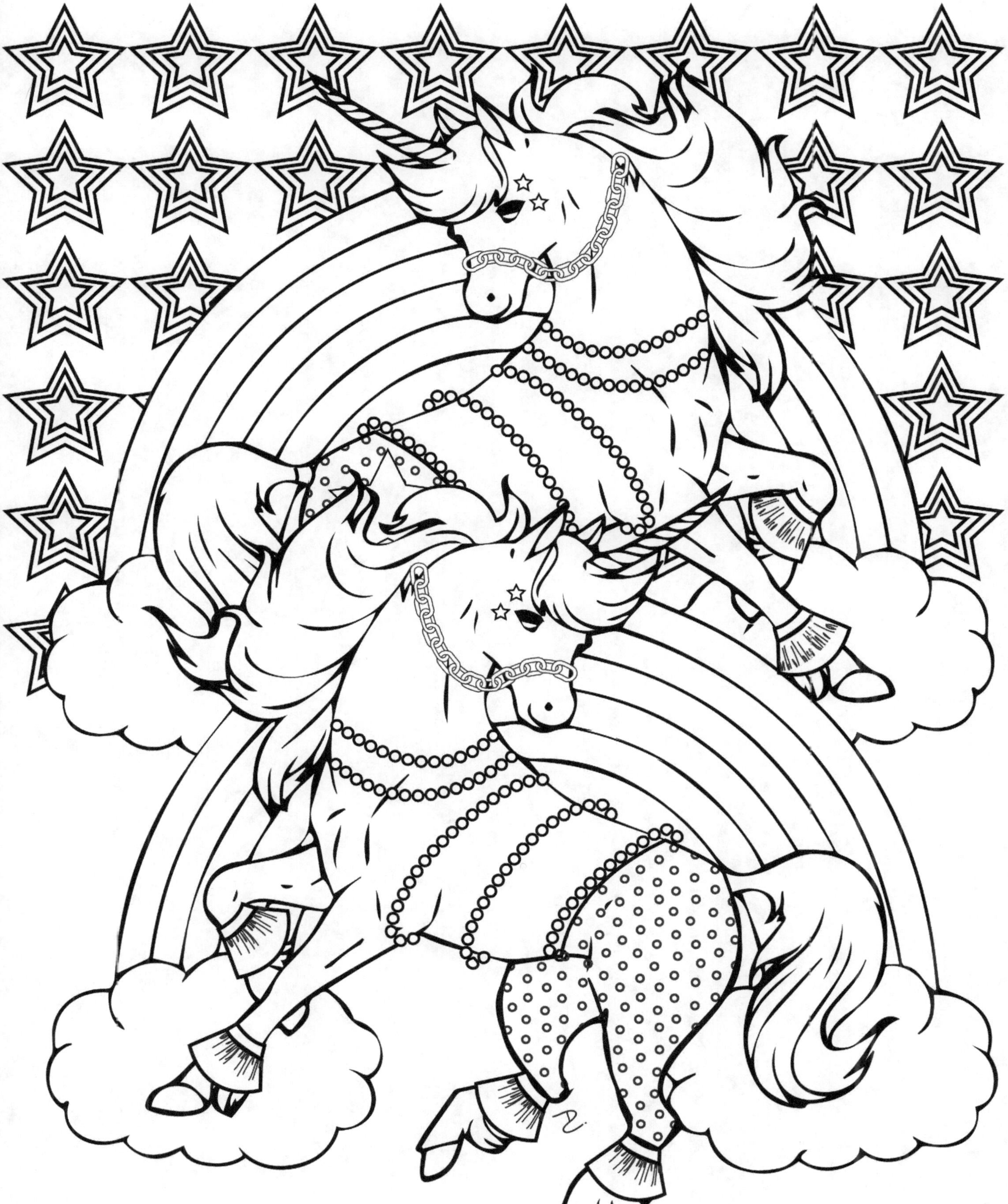

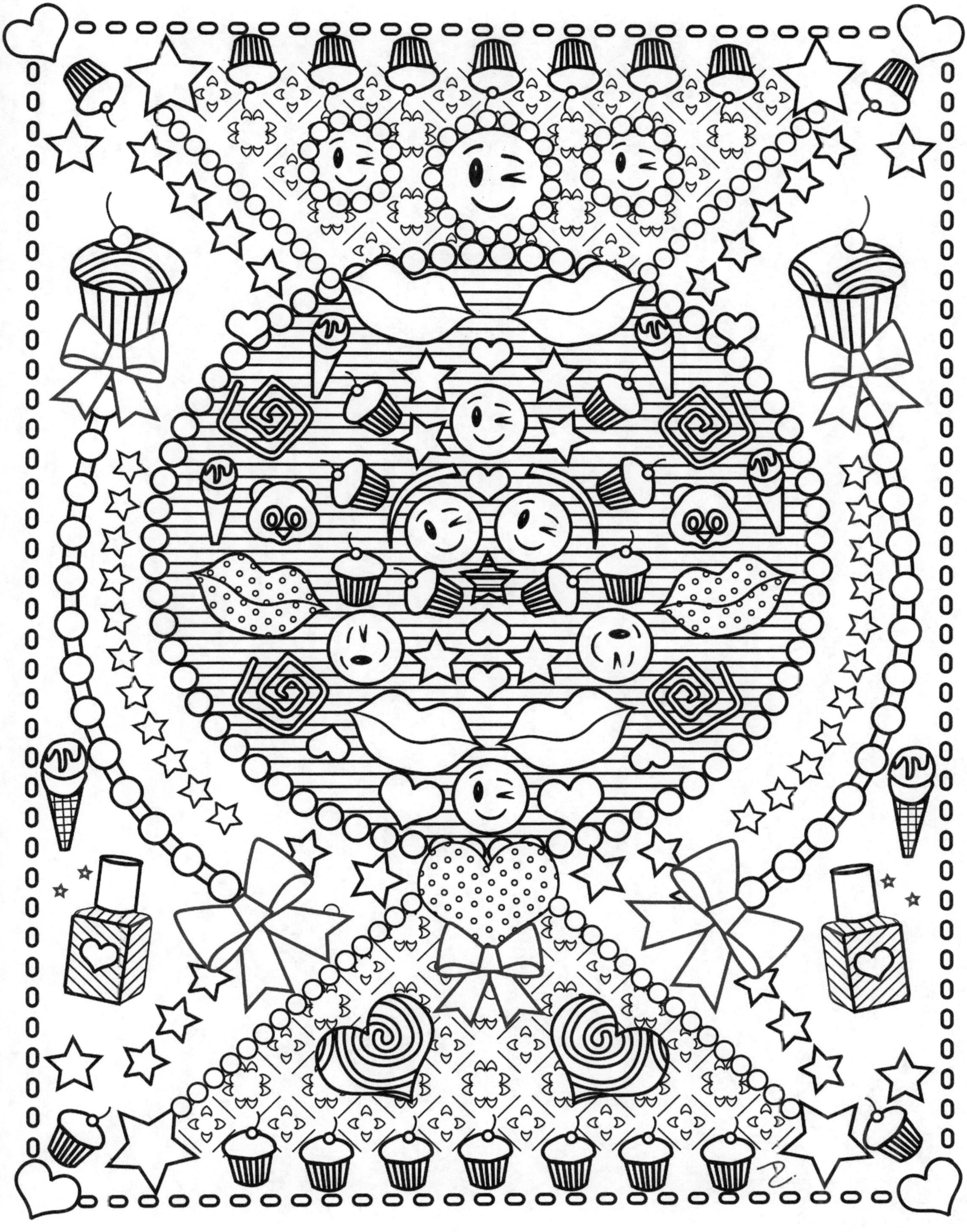

www.ingramcontent.com/pod-product-compliance
Lightning Source LLC
Chambersburg PA
CBHW080603190526
45169CB00007B/2858
* 9 7 8 1 5 2 3 9 3 6 2 1 2 *